Yellow Umbrella Books are published by Capstone Press
151 Good Counsel Drive, P.O. Box 669, Mankato, Minnesota 56002
http://www.capstone-press.com

Library of Congress Cataloging-in-Publication Data
Ring, Susan.
  The sun / by Susan Ring.
    p. cm.—(Science)
    Includes Index.
  Summary: A simple introduction to how the sun and its warmth affect the
Earth.
  ISBN 0-7368-2022-1 (hardcover : alk. paper)
  1. Photobiology–Juvenile literature. 2. Solar
radiation–Physiological effect–Juvenile literature. [1. Sun. 2. Solar
radiation.] I. Title. II. Science (Mankato, Minn.)
  QH515.R56 2003
  571.4'55–dc21

                                                              2003000923

Editorial Credits
Mary Lindeen, Editorial Director; Jennifer Van Voorst, Editor; Wanda Winch, Photo Researcher

Photo Credits
Cover: Jim Zuckerman/Corbis; Title Page: PhotoLink/PhotoDisc; Page 2: Harley D.
Nygren/NOAA; Page 3: DigitalVision; Page 4: Image Source/elektraVision; Page 5: Scott
Kerrigan/Corbis; Page 6: Mark Andersen/RubberBall Productions; Page 7: R.
Morley/PhotoLink/PhotoDisc; Page 8: Izzy Schwartz/PhotoDisc; Page 9: Jim Zuckerman/
Corbis; Page 10: David Frazier/Corbis; Page 11: Digital Vision; Page 12: Alan and Sandy
Carey/PhotoDisc; Page 13: Image Plan/Corbis; Page 14: DigitalVision; Page
15: DigitalVision; Page 16: Comstock

The Sun

by Susan Ring

Consultant: Joseph Moran, Ph.D.,
Associate Director of Education, American Meteorological Society

Yellow Umbrella Books

an imprint of Capstone Press
Mankato, Minnesota

The sun comes up.

The day begins.

The sun warms the ocean.

It helps fish grow.

The sun warms the land.

It helps flowers grow.

The sun warms the forest.

It helps trees grow.

The sun warms
the whole Earth.

The sun helps animals grow.

It helps animals stay warm,

even in cold places.

The sun warms us.

It helps us grow, too!

Good night, sun!

Words to Know/Index

animals—living creatures that can breathe and move about; pages 11, 12

Earth—the planet on which we live; page 10

flowers—colored parts of a plant that produce seeds or fruit; page 7

forest—a large area thickly covered with trees and plants; page 8

grow—to increase in size, amount, or length; pages 5, 7, 9, 11, 15

land—the part of earth's surface that is not covered by water; page 6

ocean—the body of salt water that covers most of the earth's surface; page 4

sun—the star that the earth and other planets revolve around, the sun gives light and warmth; pages 2, 4, 6, 8, 10, 11, 14, 16

trees—large, woody plants with long trunks, roots, branches, and leaves; page 9

warms—increasing the temperature of something; pages 4, 6, 8, 10, 12, 14

Word Count: 66
Early-Intervention Level: 6